Thomas Edison
토머스 에디슨

Biography Comic
who? 03 Thomas Edison

개정판 1쇄 인쇄 2014년 3월 5일
개정판 1쇄 발행 2014년 3월 10일

글 이수정
그림 스튜디오 청비
번역 자넷 재완 신
감수 김수희
펴낸이 김선식

책임편집 김선영 **디자인** 박효영
콘텐츠개발팀장 김선영 **콘텐츠개발팀** 박효영, 이유미, 김선민, 조서인
마케팅본부 이상혁

펴낸곳 스튜디오 다산 **출판등록** 2013년 11월 1일 제414-81-37694
주소 경기도 파주시 회동길 37-14 3층
전화 02-702-1724(기획편집) 02-703-1725(마케팅) 02-704-1724(경영관리)
팩스 02-703-2219 **who클럽** cafe.naver.com/dasankids
종이 월드페이퍼(주) | **인쇄** (주)현문 | **제본** 광성문화사

ISBN 979-11-5639-030-5 (14740)

• 책값은 표지 뒤쪽에 있습니다.
• 파본은 본사와 구입하신 서점에서 교환해드립니다.
• 이 책은 저작권법에 의하여 보호를 받는 저작물이므로 무단 전재와 복제를 금합니다.
• 이 책에 실린 사진의 출처는 드림스타인, 위키피디아, 연합뉴스입니다.

who?

Thomas Edison

토머스 에디슨

글 이수정 | 그림 스튜디오 청비 | 번역 자넷 재완 신 | 감수 김수희

Dasan Kid

Thomas Edison

American inventor, February 11, 1847~October 18, 1931

When Time magazine selected the most influential people of the millennium in 1998, Thomas Edison topped the list. Thomas Alva Edison was a great inventor who strove to improve the everyday life of humankind, and was born on February 11, 1847 in Milan, Ohio.

Edison possessed an unusually strong sense of curiosity, and would ask question after question to anyone who would give him their time, and he was consequently kicked out of school after only attending three months.

From then on, he was taught at home by his mother, a former school teacher, whose wise direction helped develop Edison's passion for inventions.

At the age of 22, Edison received his first patent for an electric vote-recording machine; but it was not well received by the public, causing him to taste the bitterness of failure. Afterwards, he worked on developing more practical inventions and thought up the highly successful stock ticker.

He then set up a research laboratory at his home in Menlo Park, New Jersey. Hiring engineers from various fields, he sought to develop products that would make people's lives easier. It was there that he invented the phonograph, which amazed the world and gave him the nickname "The Wizard of Menlo Park."

At the time when Thomas Edison invented the light bulb, people were using candles and oil lamps to illuminate their homes at night. He was determined to develop a cheap, high-quality light bulb that could be used in households all over America. After thousands of trials and errors, he succeeded in making the incandescent light bulb.

His inventions didn't stop there. He patented over 1,000 inventions and had a very important role in ushering in the era of electricity. His mindset of viewing failure as a mirror and a new start is to be an illumination that will stay with us forever.

토머스 에디슨

미국 발명가, 1847년 2월 11일~1931년 10월 18일

20세기 말인 1998년, 미국의 대표적인 시사 주간지 『타임』은 새로운 천 년을 맞이해서 지난 천 년 동안 인류 역사에 가장 큰 영향력을 끼친 인물 1 위 에 토머스 에디슨을 선정했습니다. 인류의 생활에 큰 혁신을 가져다 준 위대한 발명가 토머스 에디슨은 1847년 2월 11일, 미국 오하이오 주의 밀란 마을에서 태어났습니다.

유달리 호기심이 많았던 에디슨은 궁금한 것이 생기면 참지 못하고 누구에게나 질문을 쏟아 부었습니다. 입학한 지 3개월 만에 학교에서 쫓겨난 것도 그 때문이었습니다. 그 후로 에디슨은 전직 교사였던 어머니의 현명한 교육을 통해 발명에 대한 꿈을 키우며 성장해 갔습니다.

에디슨은 스물두 살에 전기 투표 기록기를 발명하여 처음으로 특허를 얻지만 사람들의 냉담한 반응에 쓰디쓴 실패를 맛보게 됩니다. 그 후 보다 실용적인 물건을 발명하기 위해 연구를 거듭한 에디슨은 주식 시세 표시기를 만들어 큰 성공을 거두었습니다.

에디슨은 뉴저지 주 멘로파크에 집과 연구소를 마련하고 여러 분야의 기술자들을 고용해 사람들의 생활을 편리하게 할 쓸모 있는 발명품을 만드는 일에 매진합니다. 그곳에서 에디슨은 축음기를 발명해 세상을 깜짝 놀라게 하며 '멘로파크의 마법사'라는 별명을 얻게 됩니다.

에디슨이 전구를 발명할 당시에는 촛불과 기름 램프가 밤을 밝히는 수단이었습니다. 에디슨은 미국의 모든 가정에서 사용할 수 있도록 값싸고 질 좋은 전구를 만들기로 결심했습니다. 수천 번의 시행착오 끝에 완성된 백열전구는 밤의 어둠을 몰아내는 데 성공합니다.

에디슨의 발명은 여기서 멈추지 않았습니다. 그는 1,000여 개가 넘는 발명품을 만들어 냈고 전기 시대를 여는 데 매우 중요한 역할을 했습니다. 실패를 거울 삼아 더욱더 노력한 에디슨의 정신은 꺼지지 않는 빛으로 우리와 영원히 함께할 것입니다.

이 책을 만든 사람들

글 · 이수정

우연히 접한 학습 만화의 매력에 푹 빠져서 어려운 내용을 어린이들의 눈높이에 맞게 쉽고 재미있게 설명할 수 있는 학습 만화 시나리오를 쓰게 되었습니다. 겉으로 보이는 위인들의 훌륭한 면뿐만 아니라 숨겨진 노력과 열정을 찾아내어 감동적인 이야기를 만들기 위해 노력합니다.

그림 · 스튜디오 청비

기발한 상상력을 바탕으로 새롭고 재미있는 콘텐츠를 만들어 내는 만화 창작 집단입니다. 어린이들이 책을 읽고 큰 꿈을 품기를 바라는 마음으로 즐겁게 작업하고 있습니다. 작품으로『성철 스님』,『아 다르고 어 다른 우리말 101가지』,『반기문 유엔 사무총장의 꿈과 도전』등이 있습니다.

번역 · 자넷 재완 신(Janet Jaywan Shin)

미국 메릴랜드 주에서 태어나고 자랐습니다. 메릴랜드 대학교에서 언어학을 전공하고 UCLA에서 응용언어학 석사 학위를 취득했습니다. 서울대학교 언어교육원에서 전임 강사, 서울대학교 사범대학교 영어교육과에서 초빙교수로 일했습니다. 감수한 책으로『서울대생한테 비밀 영어과외받기』가 있고 고등학교 영어 교과서 교정 작업에 참여했습니다.

감수 · 김수희

연세대학교에서 역사를 전공했습니다. 이후 한국뿐 아니라 일본, 미국에서 한국어, 일본어, 영어를 가르쳐 왔으며 부모를 위한 영어교육용 책을 썼습니다. 영어교육채널 EBSe '엄마표 영어특강'에서 강의를 하며 홈스쿨, 알파벳과 파닉스, 다차원 테마 영어 수업 기법을 알리고 있습니다. 전국 각지에서 어린이 영어 교육에 대한 강연을 하며 창의적이고 열정적인 교수법으로 영어를 배우고자 하는 어린이와 부모들에게 많은 도움을 주고 있습니다.

Thomas Edison

Which of the following is Edison famous for inventing and patenting?

a. Light bulb
b. Traffic light
c. Cell phone

Answer: a

Contents

01 Sitting on Eggs

 Track 01 ▶

Thomas Alva Edison was born on February 11, 1847 in Milan, Ohio.

There was another reason why the whole family had high expectations of him. They believed in folklore, which said that the seventh child would become a magician.

Come see your new little brother.

Wow! My little brother? But…

Dad, the baby's head is so big!

That means he's going to become a rich man. Hahaha!

Al, as he was called in his childhood, developed a keen sense of curiosity despite frequently falling ill.

Al! Al! Where are you?

Where did he run off to?

Edison's mother was a former school teacher, and was very wise and smart.

Al! What are you doing here?

Mom, why is that goose sitting on top of those eggs?

I guess that means I should not give up and keep going when things get tough.

Hahaha, right. But everybody has something that they're particularly good at. Mother geese are the best at brooding over their eggs. Just like the way I take care of you.

Although his first experiment didn't go the way he expected, Al was not disappointed. He was able to realize the importance of perseverance through this experiment.

I understand now.

Edison's village of Milan was always full of people bringing ships with loads of grain through the canal. Everything that Edison saw in his village peaked his curiosity.

Wow! That's incredible!

How does that big boat float in the water? I'd better ask the people who build the boats.

People began speculating that Edison was mentally handicapped, judging from his persistent and bizarre questions.

You little rascal! You've got no business asking so many questions! Scram!

Do you think that something's wrong in that kid's head?

Last time he asked if you can touch the stars if you climbed up a tree.

That's too bad. He must have something wrong with him.

When the men started to ignore Edison, he defiantly snuck into the saw mill and stole a plank of wood.

I'm going to see for myself whether or not wood floats.

Edison's intense curiosity brought about minor and major injuries, and sometimes endangered his life.

Why would the bridge sink when it's made from the same wood as boats? What went wrong?

After that big scare he'll be more careful from now on.

He's gotta learn to have some caution if he wants to stick around.

Ma, Pa, I'm sorry.

Is this something to feel sorry about?

You're lucky there was someone there to save you. From now on, you are not to go anywhere near the canal.

But Pa...

No buts! Don't even think about leaving my house anytime soon. If you do something like this again, you're really going to get it!

That's enough, dear. Al's still recovering from the shock.

He acts so wild and reckless because you let him get away with things like this! Do you know what the town people are saying about him?

Edison's upright,
but simple-minded,
father could not accept his son's
unusual inquisitive character.

SLAM

Ugh!

But Edison's mother wisely believed
that their son merely had a greater
desire to learn, compared to other children.

Mom,
am I abnormal?

No, you're
special.

Then why does
Pa hate me?

27

Thomas Alva Edison!
Do you know what you did?
You almost burned the whole
neighborhood down to
the ground!

I knew that
kid was trouble.

Edison, with his unusual curiosity,
got himself into trouble often,
but he also gained a lot of knowledge
from each experience.

02 The Best Teacher

 Track 12 ▶

When the railroad was built in Ohio, the ships stopped coming through Milan and the town population began to dwindle. As a result, Edison's father's saw mill began losing business.

A lot of people have already left town. We'd better move to another place too.

In 1854, the Edison family moved to a new house in Port Huron.

This is our new home. How do you like it?

It's great!

Yeah, it's really beautiful.

It's just like a palace, Pa!

It was a small one-room schoolhouse, run by a pastor and his wife. However, the opportunity itself to attend school was enough to excite Edison.

Unfortunately, Edison did not adjust to learning in a classroom very well and his grades were always the lowest in the class. The boring repetitive lessons could never keep Edison's attention.

Thomas! Thomas!

The wind is blowing so hard today. What if it just picks up the schoolhouse and blows it away?

The classroom, full of students of different ages mixed together, was always somewhat chaotic. During class, Edison would often doodle or stare out the window, lost in his own thoughts.

34

36

39

None of Edison's classmates felt sorry for him. They were better off not having him there to ruin the teacher's lessons.

Hehe. Good job, dummy.

Good riddance.

Now we don't have to see that moron anymore. Hehe.

In the end, Edison was kicked out of school after attending for only three months.

It's not that my child is abnormal, but that you can't understand the depth of his thinking. I don't think you are capable of educating such a gifted child.

Huh! That boy is crazy. You can't teach a crazy child.

The only person who is crazy is you. I will not let you teach my son any longer. I will take responsibility for his education!

That's fine with me. No one's stopping you.

From then on, Edison studied at home with his mother.

Of course!

Teach me more! Teach me more!

Edison enjoyed his lessons with his mother. She didn't scold him for his strange questions or punish him for not doing well on tests. She caringly worked together with him to find the answers to his questions and learn what he did wrong on tests.

Not only that, homeschooling allowed them the freedom to have class outside whenever the weather was warm.

His father had built an observation tower above Lake Huron for tourists to get a birds' eye view of the lake. Edison loved climbing up there and letting his imagination run wild.

How can humans fly like those birds?

There's no way humans can fly.

Uh-uh, uh!

Edison's power of observation would serve him well in his later research.

03 **Danger in the Lab**

 (CD1) **Track 21 ▶**

Thanks to his mother's guidance, Edison was able to learn how to read at an early age and gained vast knowledge.

What are you reading? It must be quite interesting for you not to have heard me come in.

Ah! You scared me, Mom!

The Decline and Fall of the Roman Empire? You read all of this?

Natural and Experimental Philosophy by Richard Parker is a book introducing physics, electricity, and other topics which greatly influenced Edison. He read it over and over again, and whenever he had a question, he conducted experiments to better understand the theories.

"Nature possesses an infinite number of mysterious occurrences, beyond our imagination, which are just waiting to be discovered."

As his experiments started increasing, so did the experimenting tools and chemicals in his room. He had gathered them with his friend, Michael, from various garbage dumps. Edison considered them as his precious treasures.

Michael, can you get me some salt from the kitchen?

Sure.

Edison was so happy to get his very own laboratory that he felt like he waswalking on air.

It's a powder that creates gas. It's a little bitter, but once you swallow it you'll start floating as it bubbles up. It's not scary at all.

Then you do it. I'm too scared.

I have to watch when you go up in the air and make sure you get back down safely.

Then how do I come back down?

Go near a big tree, and slowly put your arms down and stay still until you start coming down. If you wait on the tree branch, I'll bring a ladder.

Edison continued to reassure Michael until he took the powder.

With a nervous look, Michael swallowed the powder in one gulp.

Good job! Just swallow the whole vial.

Cough cough! Gross!

The taste will go away. So... do you feel the bubbling?

Yeah. I feel like throwing up.

You can't! Just wait. The gas is forming and you're going to start floating soon.

Even after a long period of time, Michael did not float.

Al, my- my stomach hurts.

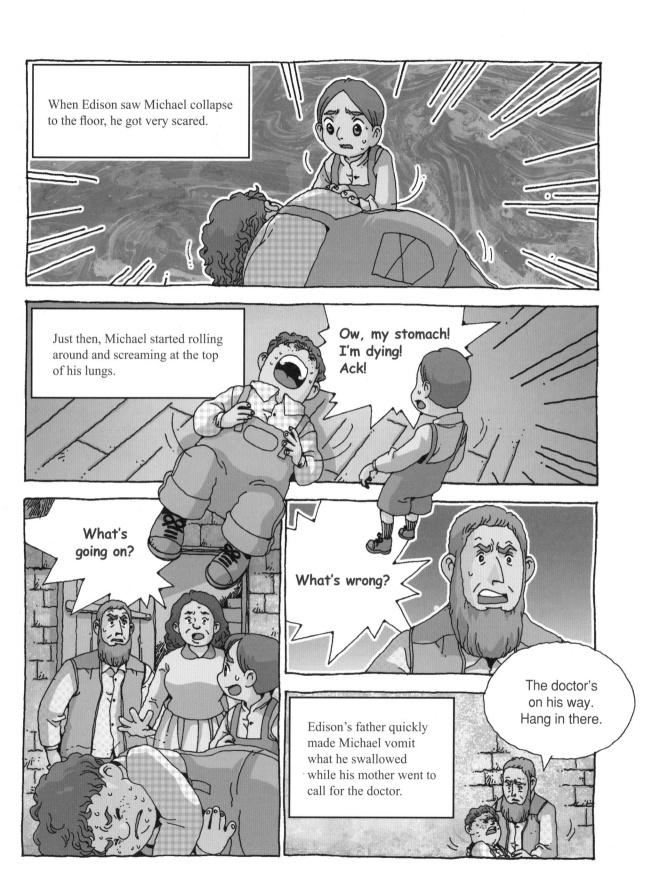

When Edison saw Michael collapse to the floor, he got very scared.

Just then, Michael started rolling around and screaming at the top of his lungs.

Ow, my stomach! I'm dying! Ack!

What's going on?

What's wrong?

Edison's father quickly made Michael vomit what he swallowed while his mother went to call for the doctor.

The doctor's on his way. Hang in there.

Edison's mother, who usually took his side, was enraged. Since she rarely got angry, her indignation was all the more fierce.

66

Everyone in town heard about Edison's experiment and was finally convinced that he was not normal.

See, that kid is not right in the head. Tsk tsk.

He wasn't kicked out of school for nothing.

That's right.

Edison was a child with a vivid imagination, but many people didn't recognize his potential. His unique imagination was his source of power to create things which no one had ever thought of, such as the telephone and the phonograph.

71

It wasn't easy to work under the hot sun. Edison's parents thought he'd give up, but he didn't and was able to raise the first harvest.

Dear, look at how much Al's grown up. He was such a troublemaker…

He has certainly grown up.

Fresh vegetables! Buy some fresh vegetables! The world's tastiest veggies are here!

You two look very young and responsible. I'll take one head of cabbage please.

Yes, ma'am.

Michael, can you bag it for her?

You got it.

04 •····· A Train Full of Hope

CD1 Track 33 ▶

Edison's business was doing better than expected, so he started selling the produce he bought from other farms. He gradually began to get the hang of running a business.

What is it?

What a perfect job!

Job Opening: Newspaper Boy on Port Huron Detroit Train

75

With his parents' approval, Edison boarded the train with a bundle of newspapers and a book in hand.

If anyone can do it, it's Al. No matter what anyone says, he's a gifted boy.

Newspaper, read all about it! Fruit, candy, and gum for sale!

Just as he expected, many passengers bought newspapers and something to eat as to pass the time.

Edison would have to wait quite a long time at the Detroit station before the Port Huron train departed. During that time, he would get more newspapers and candy to sell on the next train and go to the library and read.

I'm going to read every book in this entire library. Let's start with the ones on the bottom shelf.

It didn't take Edison long to read an entire book in one sitting, and he earned a good bit of money as well. With that money, he opened up two stands; one to sell produce and one to sell newspapers and magazines.

Michael, you've got experience selling vegetables so I'm going to let you run this stand.

What about the newspaper stand?

Are you going to do it?

No, I'm going to hire someone. I'm going to keep selling newspapers on the train.

Wow, that's brilliant.

Ha ha, good luck! The train's gonna be here soon, so see you later.

Yup.

Edison joked around and talked easily with strangers. He was no longer the kid that people used to make fun of or call mentally challenged.

84

Soon after, the world's top newspaper in those days, *The London Times*, featured an article about Edison's newspaper, *The Weekly Herald*.

These were the happiest days of Edison's youth. He was able to do everything he ever wanted.

In order to sell more newspapers, he wrote about people's private matters. After that incident, Edison quit publishing his newspaper.

I shouldn't publish gossip in the paper just to make more money. Mother would be pretty disappointed if she found out about this.

Then one day, something happened that left Edison with an injury he would never forget.

It's super bumpy today. I don't think it's safe to continue my experiment. I'd better stop...

Edison struggled to put the fire out by himself but it was getting out of control.

Just then, the conductor came in and threw a bag of sand on the fire and quenched it. Luckily, the damage was not that bad.

Whack

I told you to be careful, but look what you did.

You've been playing with dangerous chemicals this whole time? Are you crazy? Get off this train at the next station!

Unfortunately, Edison couldn't hear the conductor's last words. When he was slapped, one of his eardrums was damaged.

Even though his precious experimenting tools were cracked and broken, he gathered them all up and returned home.

What brings you home so early, son?

What did you say, Mother? Can you speak louder? I can't hear you very well.

Why are you yelling like that?

Your voice is so soft
I can't hear you!

Sensing the seriousness of the situation,
Edison's mother took him
to see a doctor.

What do you
mean he can't
hear?

Something happened to
his ear when he got hit.
Because the eardrum
has been damaged,
his hearing cannot
be restored.

There must be some way.
Please tell me
there's a way.

…

I'm sorry. But the other ear
is functioning,
so he shouldn't have
any problems going
about his normal
daily life.

Edison was able to overcome the reality of his handicap through the help of his wise mother.

Watch my lips carefully! You've got good observation skills so you're going to adjust in no time.

Ok.

Did you know that Beethoven also lost his hearing? Can you imagine how hard it was for a musician to go deaf? Nevertheless, he was able to create beautiful music that moved so many people.

...but Beethoven was gifted.

Did you hear everything I said?

I only heard about half of what you said, so don't get so excited.

Good. You're halfway there. If you make some effort, you can overcome it!

There's something wrong with his head.

You're an idiot!

That's right. This is only a minor crisis. I can overcome this.

05 Failure Comes Before Success

Edison was adjusting to his new life through the devoted efforts of his mother. Even though he couldn't hear very well in one ear, he lived more diligently than ever before.

It's a good thing that you quit. Is everything else alright?

Yeah, I am getting by just fine! Haha.

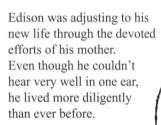

Jimmie! Watch out!

One day at the railroad station, he saw the station agent's son in danger. Edison saw a train coming from the opposite direction and jumped onto the tracks to save the child.

To Edison's surprise,
he was offered the position of telegraph
operator as a reward for his heroic act.
Edison, who loved anything new,
didn't miss the opportunity to learn
the telegraph. It was the latest
technology of that time, and the telegraph
was the fastest mode of communication.

You can send letters
or numbers by
changing them into
electric signals.

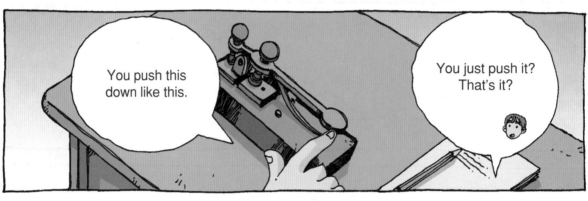

You push this
down like this.

You just push it?
That's it?

No, the length of time
you push it down is different
for each letter.
The same is also true
for numbers.

It's like
a secret code.

Edison worked hard and earned
his telegraph operating license
at the age of 16. Some time later,
a telegraph station in Port Huron
was set up.

The station soon closed due to a lack of telegraph operators. Upon hearing of a job opening at Stratford Junction, he headed for Canada and got the job.

We have to send the message "6" once every hour to Toronto's chief engineer.

What does that mean?

It tells them we're still here. It gets awfully quiet here at night since there are almost no trains. Why did you choose the night shift?

I have to study during the day.

If you fall asleep and miss a signal, you're out of a job. You hear me?

Yes, sir.

Zzzz Zzzz

I can't keep falling asleep like this. What should I do?

Edison had to change jobs many times before he was even 20 years old. It became a routine for him to get fired from jobs after conducting experiments at work or trying to reconstruct the telegraph machine.

Edison could not get hired anywhere anymore, so he returned to his hometown penniless. When he saw how much his parents had aged and how shabby their home had gotten, he became determined to earn the money needed to support them.

I can't see my parents in this state. I should be helping them, not causing trouble. I've got to make some money so that I can offer some support.

With the help of a friend from Boston, he got hired at a telegraph station and worked diligently.

That hillbilly over there got a special appointment?

They say his skills are pretty remarkable.

I think it's despicable how that country boy walks around acting like he knows it all.

That guy's in charge of New York communications, isn't he?

Quick Rick! The guy who sends the fastest telegrams in New York.

That's it. As good as his skills might be, he's no match for Quick Rick.

Telegrams were coming in from New York just like any other day when suddenly the speed of the telegram quickened. Edison was momentarily surprised, but kept pace easily.

What is this?
He's getting it all correct, down to the last letter.

We underestimated his skills.

Then one day, Edison read Michael Faraday's "Experimental Researches in Electricity" and became fascinated with his innovative electricity research. Faraday had a big influence on sparking Edison's interest in electricity.

You're reading that book again? Enough is enough. You haven't been eating or sleeping for days.

You've got to take better care of yourself.

This book contains all the experiments that I want to do. I wish there were more than twenty-four hours in a day.

You're doing plenty already. All of your waking hours are spent either working or experimenting.

It's not enough. Reading this, I realize how little I really do know. If I don't research and experiment harder, it's not going to be enough.

105

What about work? You need to earn money to live. Your research doesn't earn you money.

No! It can earn me money.

In 1869, Edison, at the age of 22, decides to become an inventor.

There isn't enough time in the day for all the experiments I want to do.

That's right. I think I'd better quit telegraph work. I'm going to do what I really want to do from now on!

Here's the Capitol building. Let's go inside.

Inside the Capitol building, Edison saw a long line of congressmen waiting to make their vote.

It's going to take forever to record all of their votes.

They should just be able to press a button from their seats.

That's how Edison's first invention came into existence. Edison firmly believed his electric vote recorder would make the voting process less cumbersome by reducing the voting time.

Edison was quite disappointed that the invention he put his whole fortune into was found to be useless. However his passion for inventing did not change.

Edison moved to New York where there were other inventors.
He decided that he wanted to work for Dr. Rose, the inventor of the gold market ticker.

He had no more money and no place to go, so he hid in Dr. Rose's company building. During the day, he would examine their machines and he would sleep in the basement by night.

What they do here is amazing! I definitely want to work for this company.

On the fourth day Edison was there, one of the machines that had been working well suddenly broke down. The customers were outraged while the engineers desperately tried to find the source of the problem. This crisis almost forced the company to go out of business.

Can I give it a shot?

Excuse me?
Do you know how to handle this machine?

WHIRRR

Boy, how do you know how to operate the gold market ticker?

Edison was completely dumbfounded when the man offered him such an exorbitant amount, far beyond what he was expecting. He never imagined that he'd be able to see that much money in his lifetime.

Is that too low?

N-No. That'll be fine.

The first person he told the good news to was his mother.

Dear Mother,
How are you? Things have been going well,
and I am planning to set up my own laboratory soon.
I hope you will get better by the time the lab
is complete so that you can come and see it.
Don't push yourself too hard,
and if you ever need help,
please let me know anytime.

In 1870, Edison set up his laboratory in Newark, New Jersey. However, his mother passed away before she could see her son's achievement.

His mother always encouraged and believed in him, and he wept with regret at not being able to be with her during her final hour.

Oh, Mother!

Thomas Edison, the father of inventions, might never have existed if it weren't for his mother's encouragement and confidence in his abilies.

Mary Stilwell, at the age of sixteen, helped Edison through this hard time. The sensitive young woman reached out with warmth and understanding.

Oh, I'm sorry. I was just trying to get out of the rain.

It was love at first sight, and they were wed on Christmas Day of that year.

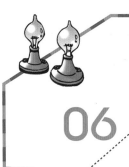

06

The Wizard of Menlo Park

Five years later, In addition, his laboratory, which began with five employees, was now fifty times bigger and divided into five different labs.

Edison slept for only four hours a night and continued to work hard, earning the trust and respect of his employees. The laboratory in Newark was getting cramped so in 1876, Edison established a bigger lab and home in Menlo Park, New Jersey. The first thing Edison did in his new lab was improve the telephone.

Didn't Alexander Graham Bell already invent the telephone? Why do we want to fix someone else's invention? In my opinion, the telephone seems flawless.

I think that making a good thing even better is part of our work.

There are numerous inconveniences with Bell's telephone.

There's only one transmitter-receiver, so you must put it to your mouth to speak, and then put it to your ear to listen. That is quite cumbersome. Hence, it is impossible to talk at the same time as the person on the other end.

In addition, the magnetic device between the receiver and the wire cannot pick up the softer sounds.

Edison conducted thousands of trials, but he was not satisfied with the results. His notebooks were only getting filled with details of the tests.

The connection between the diaphragm and the wire needs to be strong. What material could work?

This is when Edison's habit of taking notes began. When inspiration came to mind, he would write it down immediately, even if he was in the middle of his meal or sleeping. All of the notes he recorded in his lifetime fill up an unbelievable five million pages.

This is it!

What are you planning to do with that soot, sir?

These carbon particles can change the electric current that is produced when we speak.

Carbon?

The main component of soot!

In 1878, Edison was able to connect with a telephone more than 300 kilometers away. The other person's voice came through clearly, and the trial was a success.

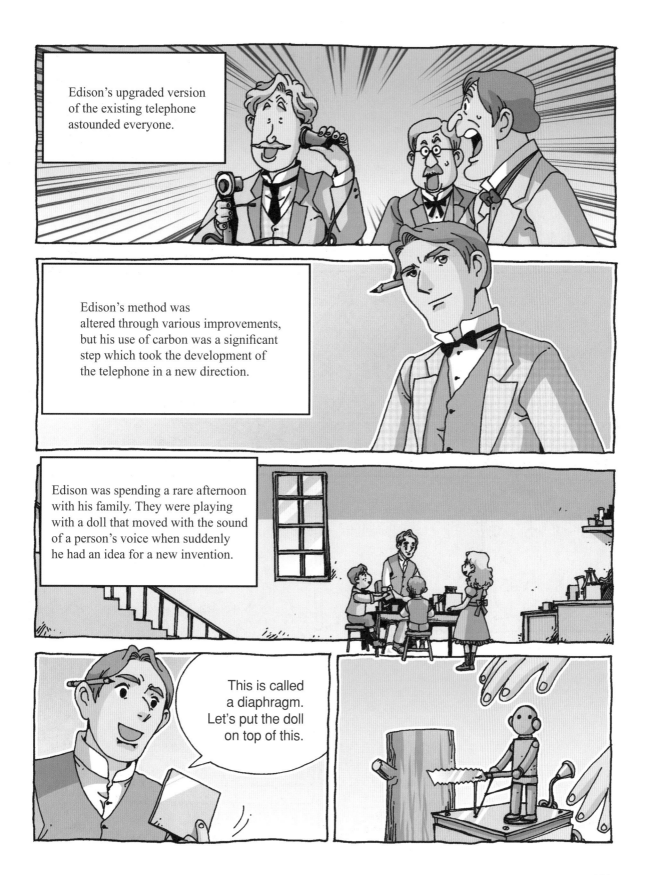

Edison's upgraded version of the existing telephone astounded everyone.

Edison's method was altered through various improvements, but his use of carbon was a significant step which took the development of the telephone in a new direction.

Edison was spending a rare afternoon with his family. They were playing with a doll that moved with the sound of a person's voice when suddenly he had an idea for a new invention.

This is called a diaphragm. Let's put the doll on top of this.

Edison suddenly realized that if the doll could move at the sound of a voice, then it must be possible to change that movement back into sound.

Edison drew up the blueprint in an instant and gave it to John Kruesi, who constructed mechanical devices.

Kruesi took a look at the blueprint of a machine with a handle that goes round and round, a cylinder with a groove carved in it, and a needle and diaphragm attached on either end. He was befuttled.

What in the world does this do?

It's a talking machine.

Edison paid no attention to his workers' ridicule, and started to turn the handle again.

Then the rhyme that Edison just recited started to flow out of the machine. It was clearly his voice.

What- What in the world?

Everyone, taken completely aback, just stared mesmerized at the machine. Edison couldn't believe it himself. Usually it takes a long period of time and many failures before an invention will work, but this one worked the very first time.

I don't believe it. This is the most amazing machine I have ever seen.

Truly incredible!

Mr. Edison, I love you!

This was the invention of the phonograph, a machine which could surpass time and place. Edison, who could only hear in one ear, gave the beautiful gift of music to the world.

When Edison's invention of the phonograph became known to the public, America and the whole world was buzzing. Edison and the phonograph were on the front page of newspapers day after day, and people even began gathering at Edison's lab.

Major Invention Creates a New Chapter in History!

Edison the Magician! Talking Machine Invented!

Is He God or is He Human?

He was even invited to the White House to demonstrate the phonograph to the president.

At one point, Edison began to be known as "the Wizard of Menlo Park".

However, Edison wasn't particularly satisfied with this turn of events.

07 Lighting Up the Darkness

Edison returned from his travels full of vision. People in those days would use candles or oil lamps at night for light. Now Edison poured all his energy into inventing the light bulb.

Isn't there already a lamp that uses electricity?

Of course there is the arc lamp. But it's expensive and the hot sparks that fly out are very dangerous. It might be fine for outdoors, but it's not suitable as an indoor lamp. I am going to make a safe electric light that can be used inside.

Many scientists have studied how to use electricity to create light before, but there has yet to be any significant results reported. It's going to require a lot of time and money.

And a lot of effort as well. I am determined to make an electric light for homes that is both inexpensive and easy to use.

I know it's going to be hard and we may not complete this, but we've already begun so we must move forward. If my workers see me wavering and unsure, they'll falter too.

Edison acted as if he had already invented the light bulb, but some of his engineers were turning against him.

This is nonsense!

I don't know what kind of trick he's going to use to accomplish something that other scientists could only dream of.

He acts so confident, as if he's already invented the light bulb.

You know, they say the ignorant are the brave ones.

Ignorance has its limits, you know. Does he think he can just force his agenda every time?

He's not right in his mind.

If I keep working for an insane man like him, I think I'll go mad too. I quit. I can't work here anymore.

Edison began by recruiting workers who believed in his vision. He also started seeking advice from scientists who had previously attempted to make light bulbs.

In addition, Edison gathered newspaper reporters from New York together to make a serious announcement.

I am going to make an inexpensive and practical light that uses electricity. You will soon experience a new world where only the rich will burn candles.

At that time, expensive electric lamps were used only by the rich. They were also inconvenient and dangerous, and could not be used in homes. When the sun set at the end of the day, people were forced to head home and prepare for bed. Edison wanted to make an inexpensive light so that the average person could read and study at night.

Since Edison was already well-known for the invention of the phonograph, people had great expectations of him and donated a lot of money to support his research.

He's an amazing man.

Edison the Wizard, This Time the Light Bulb!

I really hope he can succeed with the light bulb invention.

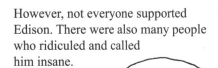

However, not everyone supported Edison. There were also many people who ridiculed and called him insane.

College? He didn't even go to elementary school. He got expelled!

Hmph. Look at this conceited fool. He's not even a college graduate.

It figures that someone with hardly any education would babble like he does. Maybe he's really got something wrong with his head.

Edison built a new research lab where they could concentrate on inventing the light bulb. He also recruited new scholars excelling in mathematics and science, as well as skilled glass blowers and metal workers.

The biggest problem is making a filament that emits light inside the glass bulb while electricity is flowing.

We have to test everything, no matter what the material is. I don't care if is metal, paper, food, or textiles. Don't make a judgment before you actually test it.

138

If we can solve those problems, then we can use platinum for the filament.

Platinum has the ability to expand, so we can make a very thin filament with it. We just need to make a vacuum pump to take the air out from the inside of the bulb!

Ah, that'll work. Ha ha ha.

Incidentally, making the platinum filament was a failure. The experiments using the expensive metal cost them fifty thousand dollars, drying up their research funds. They needed more money to continue research.

Then let us see the results of the study that you've spent all that money on.

We don't have results from the study yet.

But you must have something. You used fifty thousand dollars' worth of platinum, there must have been something you gained from it.

But…

We have a right to know.

Yes, sir.

When Edison brought out the light bulbs, people had high expectations that they would shine brightly, but the bulbs only lit up for a very short moment and went dark.

143

We beg you!

Gentlemen, why don't we give them some more time? These are young men in their prime, confined to the lab all day long.

With this much perseverance and focus, these men are going to accomplish something, no matter how long it takes.

Edison succeeded in changing the minds of the investors by earnestly pleading with them, but he soon fell ill. His eyes had developed a condition from looking at bright light for long periods of time while testing filaments.

For the time being, you must stop doing your experiments.

I cannot do that. Doctor, I do not have much time.

If you continue to get exposed to that light, you could go blind!

Edison was inspired when he saw soot and came upon the idea of using carbon. He was finally able to make a carbonized yarn by covering it with carbon powder at a high temperature. Everyone in the lab focused on making a carbon filament and after a week, they were able to make three.

Finally the great experiment that marked a new civilization had begun.

Let's start.

GULP

Edison inserted the filament inside the bulb, pumped the air out to create a vacuum state, and turned on the electric current. The filament began to glow brightly. It was a sign of the most innovative change in the history of humankind.

So far, it's the same as all of our other trials. This too will probably flicker and die, as so many previous lamps have done.

Well, let's see.

I can't watch. If this one fails, then I don't know...

Why don't you go home for the night?

Two hours have passed!

Yes. Let's keep watching a bit longer.

Time passed by,
but the light continued to beam.
The next morning,
the light was still on when
the men came back to work.

The age of the light bulb had finally arrived. It was now possible to read, study, and work at night.

We did it!

Yes!

When the investors heard that the light bulb was completed, they urged him to have it manufactured into a commercial product as quickly as possible.
Edison, however, wanted to work on it more and refused their demands.

How long are you going to keep researching?

That's right. We've given you this much time and money, it's time we got something in return.

We'll have plenty of time to manufacture and sell it after we've perfected it.

You are obsessed with perfection. It's taken fifteen months to make this light bulb!

Edison began to look again for a new material for the filament. In the process, he learned that using bamboo would lengthen the life of the bulb.

In order to find good quality bamboo, Edison sent his researchers to Asia, Africa, and South America, and found out that bamboo in Japan was the most suitable for his purposes.

After persistent effort, they made a bulb that lasted for 170 hours. Edison told the newspaper reporters that on the last night of 1879, he would present the incandescent light bulb to the public.

Wizard Edison Overcomes Darkness
Light Bulb Invented!
To Be Unveiled at Menlo Park, December 31st, 1879

Finally,
the darkness of the night disappeared in Menlo Park.

There was still more work left for Edison. In order for the light bulb to actually be used, it required a plug, switch, fuse, socket and other attachments.

Men, let's hang in there for a little longer. We can't give up on the light bulb. We've put our sweat, blood, and tears into it's creation!

Yes, sir!

I want to make our light bulb so that everyone in the world can use it. Let's work on this a little longer!

Edison set up an electric light company in New York in 1881, and began to work on an electric generator.

Mr. Edison, you got an invitation to an electrical exhibition in Paris.

I have too much work here to do.

They're requesting that you attend. Even if you're busy, I think you should make the time to go.

Have you forgotten that we have to install electric lights in New York City? Electrical exhibitions are important, but work is our first priority. Let's go next time.

Yes, sir.

Tell them that we'll send them lighting and a generator to display in their exhibition hall.

Yes, sir.

On September 4, 1882, the six generators that Edison built for New York City were in full operation. Electricity flowed through twenty-two kilometers of wire to 85 homes, to illuminate 400 lights all at once and emit a beautiful radiance.

The mood was festive in New York City on that historical night. Edison claimed that he would make it easy for anyone to use electric light, and his vision became a reality.

153

08

Remembered as the Everlasting Light

Edison did not attend the electrical exhibition, but he did receive the honor of the highest prize for his lights, which beat out all the competition.

When news spread about Edison winning, he began to receive letters from all over the world. Some were investors and people concerned with patent issues. He also became incredibly busy, creating several businesses related to electric light.

In the midst of all this, Edison's family was left neglected. Mary passed away on that very day, leaving him and their young children.

Dear, I'm sorry.

Edison decided to close the research lab at Menlo Park, where memories of his wife lingered everywhere.

Mary!

In order to escape the pain of losing his wife, Edison immersed himself in his work even more than usual.

After some time passed, Edison was introduced by a friend to the daughter of another inventor, Mina Miller.

Hey! I was reading that!

Do you know how many hours I waited? I've lived for twenty years as the daughter of an inventor, but I've never seen the likes of you!

Two years later, Edison married Mina Miller and established their new home and his research lab in West Orange, New Jersey.

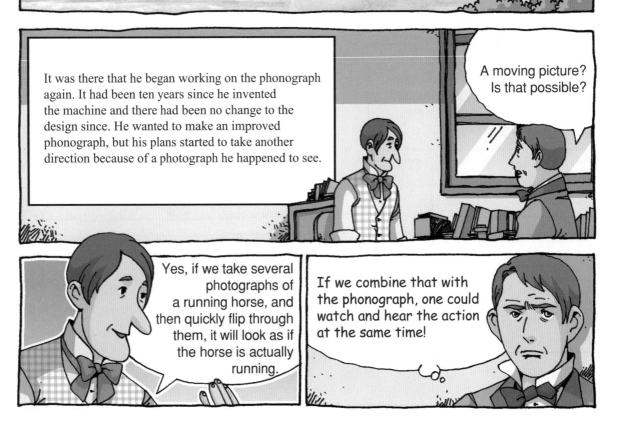

It was there that he began working on the phonograph again. It had been ten years since he invented the machine and there had been no change to the design since. He wanted to make an improved phonograph, but his plans started to take another direction because of a photograph he happened to see.

A moving picture? Is that possible?

Yes, if we take several photographs of a running horse, and then quickly flip through them, it will look as if the horse is actually running.

If we combine that with the phonograph, one could watch and hear the action at the same time!

Fifty years before Hollywood began producing films with audio dialogue, Edison had already thought of the idea when no one had even fathomed the concept of a movie.
His invention of the phonograph was what sparked his imagination.

He invented the movie camera (the kinetograph) placed it in his moving picture projector (the kinetoscope) which projected them onto a small screen inside the machine.
This was how the movie first came to life.

In the course of improving the phonograph several times and inventing the movie camera, microscope, storage battery, and many other things,
Edison became a gray-haired elderly man.

157

Sir, it's time for us to leave.

Alright.

On October 21, 1929, there was a celebration to commemorate fifty years since the invention of the light bulb and honor Edison's achievements.
There was still a lot of time before the event began, but Edison still rushed to Greenfield, Michigan.

Ah, Henry! You're already here. Good to see you.

You must be worn out from all the traveling.

So now you're treating me like an old person.

Ha ha ha. Not at all.

Henry Ford, the father of the automobile, shared a special history with Edison.
They had met in their younger days when Ford worked at Edison's lab.
For this special occasion, Ford brought to Greenfield a replica of the train on which Edison used to sell newspapers and candy.

Oh my goodness! This train is still around!

When Edison saw the cargo car, his tears started to fall. There was a shelf full of chemicals, experiment equipment, the newspaper printing press, and a box stuffed with newspapers and candy; just like in his youth.

It looks just like my old cargo car!

Why don't you show us your skills?

Eighty-year old Thomas Edison felt as if he went back in time.

Newspapers, read all about it! Candy and gum for sale!

Rattle

Fire! Fire!

Oh rats, I'm going to get fired again.

Young Edison had been kicked off the train, but Elderly Edison was safely helped off by the President of the United States, Herbert Hoover.

Not only was there the train from Edison's youth, but there was an exact recreation of his Menlo Park lab and surrounding streets. When Edison went inside, he inspected it thoroughly.

This is where it all happened.

Mr. Edison!

Oh, why it's Francis!

The two gray-haired elderly men began to re-enact how they made the light bulb in their youth.

160

After his speech, Edison, whose health had been failing, suddenly collapsed. Edison was quickly moved to another room to receive medical attention.

You needn't worry. I just got overwhelmed by all the memories from the past.

Edison lived two more years after that event. On October 18, 1931, eighty-four year old Edison quietly closed his eyes.

On the night of Edison's funeral,
at ten o'clock, lights began to turn off
one by one. All over America,
the pitch-black darkness settled in.

This was done in memory of Thomas Edison as people mourned his death.

Thomas Alva Edison, the genius of hard work!
He asked questions about everything in the world,
was full of curiosity about anything new,
never afraid of failure.
The inventions of
Thomas Alva Edison,
which we cannot live without,
are the great legacy that
he has left behind.

If it wasn't for him, we wouldn't be able to listen to
beautiful music whenever, wherever we wanted.
There would be no light to illuminate the night,
and there would be no movies.
Edison was an innovator who continued to
research and experiment even after he already
invented hundreds of inventions we use each day.
This is due to his perseverance, thousands
of failures, and endless efforts.
Edison created a new civilization with his inventions
and will be remembered eternally as a brilliant light.

Word Search

● Find the words which are hidden horizontally, vertically and diagonally.

Q	M	Z	G	Q	M	Z	G	Q	M	Z	G	Q	Q	M	Z	G	Q	M	I
W	I	A	H	W	N	A	H	W	N	A	H	W	N	A	H	W	N	M
E	N	Q	J	E	B	Q	J	E	B	Q	J	E	E	B	Q	J	N	B	P
R	C	C	K	I	N	T	E	N	S	E	K	R	R	V	C	O	R	V	R
T	A	D	L	T	C	D	L	T	C	D	L	T	T	C	I	L	T	C	O
Y	N	E	Q	Y	X	E	Q	Y	X	E	Q	Y	Y	S	E	P	Y	X	V
U	D	W	U	P	V	W	U	Z	V	W	U	S	Z	V	H	U	Z	E
I	E	R	E	I	A	A	E	I	A	R	E	A	I	A	R	O	I	A	M
O	S	G	R	O	S	G	T	O	S	G	P	O	O	S	G	N	O	S	E
P	C	H	T	P	D	H	T	E	D	H	T	P	P	D	H	O	P	D	N
A	E	U	Y	A	F	U	Y	A	N	U	Y	A	A	F	U	G	A	F	T
S	N	I	U	S	G	I	U	S	G	T	U	S	S	G	I	R	S	G	I
D	T	O	I	D	H	O	I	D	H	O	I	D	D	H	O	A	D	H	O
F	J	T	J	F	J	T	J	F	J	T	J	F	F	J	T	P	F	J	T
G	K	S	B	G	K	S	B	G	K	S	B	G	G	K	S	H	G	K	S
H	L	E	N	H	L	E	N	H	L	E	N	H	H	L	E	N	H	L	E
J	Q	T	M	J	Q	T	I	L	L	U	M	I	N	A	T	E	J	Q	T
L	W	Y	Q	L	W	Y	Q	L	W	Y	Q	L	L	W	Y	Q	L	W	Y
Z	W	K	F	Z	W	K	F	Z	W	K	F	Z	Z	W	K	F	Z	W	K
X	E	M	U	X	E	M	U	X	E	M	U	X	X	E	M	U	X	E	M
C	R	D	E	V	E	L	O	P	M	E	N	T	C	R	Q	C	C	R	Q

passion	patent	incandescent	intense
improvement	development	phonograph	illuminate

Lesson 2 Vocabulary

● Match each word to the correct meaning.

1. curiosity   • 이루다

2. bizarre   •탄소

3. accomplish   • 호기심

4. convenient   • 인내력

5. eardrum   • 별난

6. innovative   • 혁신적인

7. usher   • 소란

8. civilization   • 안내하다

9. perseverance   • 고막

10. uproar   • 문명

11. concentration   • 집중

12. carbon   • 편리한

Guess What?

Lesson 3

● Guess what he said in the blank.

My Own Invention!

• Create your own inventions. And describe it.

1. What is your invention's name?

_____

2. What does the name mean?

_____

3. What is it used for?

_____

4. How big is this invention?

_____

5. Draw your invention in the box below.

Lesson 5
The Phonograph

   While Thomas Edison was trying to invent a telephone that performed better than Alexander Graham Bell's invention, he came upon the idea of the phonograph. He thought that if it was possible to convert a voice into vibration, movement, then it should be possible to conversely convert that movement into sound. When Edison played back the sounds he had recorded on the phonograph, the Menlo Park researchers were astounded. At the time, it was unimaginable to think that one could record sound.

   Because of the invention of the phonograph, music records were able to be produced and people were able to enjoy music whenever they wanted. But it is said that Edison was not actually planning to make a machine related with music. He wanted the phonograph to be like an audio book that the blind could listen to. Edison is said to have loved the phonograph the most out of all his inventions.

에디슨과 그가 발명한 축음기

미시건 주 그린필드에 옛 모습 그대로 재현된
멘로파크 연구소

6 The Light Bulb

Thomas Edison knew that no matter how good an invention might be, if it was not practical, then it was useless. After testing more than six thousand kinds of materials, he found that using a bamboo filament would increase the life span of the light bulb considerably. The bamboo filament was the best material, allowing the bulb to stay lit safely for more than one thousand hours.

On December 31, 1879, Edison presented the incandescent light bulb to the public in Menlo Park. Once the light bulb was introduced, the world, not to mention America, was ecstatic. Thomas Edison was praised as the great inventor who gave light to humanity and the world became able to illuminate the night brightly.

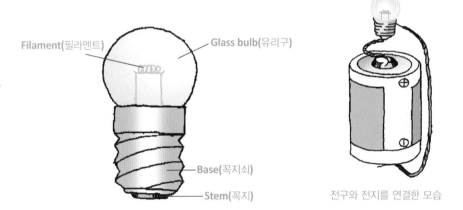

Filament(필라멘트)　　　Glass bulb(유리구)

Base(꼭지쇠)

Stem(꼭지)

전구와 전지를 연결한 모습

- Glass bulb : The round glass shape which protects the filament.
- Filament : The spring part from which light emanates.
- Base : Connected with a wire from the filament which is surrounded by the bulb.
- Stem : Connected with another wire which comes from the filament out of the base.

연표

1847년   2월 11일, 미국 오하이오 주 밀란에서 태어났습니다.

1854년 7세   미시간 주 포트 휴런으로 이사합니다.

1855년 8세   초등학교에 입학하지만 석 달 만에 쫓겨나 어머니로부터 교육을
             받게 됩니다.

1857년 10세 지하실에 자신의 실험실을 만들고 파커의 입문서 등을 참고로
             실험에 몰두합니다.

1859년 12세 포트 휴런과 디트로이트를 잇는 그랜드 트렁크 철도의 신문 판매원으로
             일합니다.

1862년 15세 세계 최초의 차내 신문 『위클리 헤럴드』를 발행합니다.
             전신 기사 자격증을 획득하고 포트 휴런에 작은 전신국을 차립니다.

1863년 16세 그랜드 트렁크 철도의 야간 통신사로 취직하지만 사고를 일으켜 해고
             당합니다.

1869년 22세 발명가의 길을 걷기로 결심한 후, 처음으로 전기 투표 기록기를 발명
             하여 첫 특허를 받습니다. 이후 금 시세 표시기의 개량형인 주식 시세
             표시기를 발명해 많은 돈을 법니다.

1870년 23세 뉴저지 주의 뉴어크에 공장을 짓고 전기 기구의 연구를 시작합니다.

1871년 24세 메리 스틸엘과 결혼합니다.

1876년 29세 멘로파크에 연구소를 설립하고 탄소 송화기를 개발합니다.

1877년 30세 축음기를 발명합니다.

1878년 31세 백악관에서 미국 과학 학회 회원들과 대통령 앞에서 축음기를
선보입니다.

1879년 32세 탄소 필라멘트를 사용한 백열전구를 발명합니다.
멘로파크에서 최초로 백열전구를 공개합니다.

1880년 33세 에디슨 전구 회사를 세웁니다.

1881년 34세 파리에서 열린 전기 박람회에서 최고 상인 레종 도뇌르 명예상을
수상합니다.

1882년 35세 뉴욕 시 월 가에 발전기를 설치하고 400개의 전구를 밝힙니다.

1884년 37세 메리가 병으로 세상을 떠나자 멘로파크 연구소를 폐쇄합니다.

1887년 40세 미나 밀러와 재혼한 후, 웨스트 오렌지에 연구소를 세웁니다.

1889년 42세 키네토그래프를 발명합니다.

1891년 44세 철광석의 자력 선광법을 연구해 자력 선광기를 발명합니다.

1895년 48세 X선용 투시경을 발명합니다.

1909년 62세 알칼리 축전지를 발명합니다.

1912년 65세 축음기와 활동사진을 연결한 키네토폰을 발명합니다.

1929년 82세 백열전구 발명 50주년 기념 행사에서 연설 도중 쓰러집니다.

1931년 84세 10월 18일, 84세의 나이로 생을 마감합니다.

who? 01	Barack Obama	979-11-5639-023-7
who? 02	Charles Darwin	979-11-5639-024-4
who? 03	Bill Gates	979-11-5639-025-1
who? 04	Hillary Clinton	979-11-5639-026-8
who? 05	Stephen Hawking	979-11-5639-027-5
who? 06	Oprah Winfrey	979-11-5639-028-2
who? 07	Steven Spielberg	979-11-5639-029-9
who? 08	Thomas Edison	979-11-5639-030-5
who? 09	Abraham Lincoln	979-11-5639-031-2
who? 10	Martin Luther King, Jr.	979-11-5639-032-9
who? 11	Louis Braille	979-11-5639-033-6
who? 12	Albert Einstein	979-11-5639-034-3
who? 13	Jane Goodall	979-11-5639-035-0
who? 14	Walt Disney	979-11-5639-036-7
who? 15	Winston Churchill	979-11-5639-037-4
who? 16	Warren Buffett	979-11-5639-008-4
who? 17	Nelson Mandela	979-11-5639-009-1
who? 18	Steve Jobs	979-11-5639-010-7
who? 19	J. K. Rowling	979-11-5639-011-4
who? 20	Jean-Henri Fabre	979-11-5639-012-1
who? 21	Vincent van Gogh	979-11-5639-013-8
who? 22	Marie Curie	979-11-5639-014-5
who? 23	Henry David Thoreau	979-11-5639-015-2
who? 24	Andrew Carnegie	979-11-5639-016-9
who? 25	Coco Chanel	979-11-5639-017-6
who? 26	Charlie Chaplin	979-11-5639-018-3
who? 27	Ho Chi Minh	979-11-5639-019-0
who? 28	Ludwig van Beethoven	979-11-5639-020-6
who? 29	Mao Zedong	979-11-5639-021-3
who? 30	Kim Dae-jung	979-11-5639-022-0